The Final Journey

of

Joseph Cardinal Bernardin

The Final Journey

of

Joseph Cardinal Bernardin

Photography of John H. White

Contributors:

Most Rev. Raymond E. Goedert, D.D.

Rev. Msgr. Kenneth Velo

Sr. Mary Brian Costello, R.S.M.

Sr. Mary Lucia Skalka, C.S.S.F.

Dr. Ellen Gaynor, O.P., M.D.

 Loyola Press

Photographs taken on assignment by John H. White are reprinted with permission from the *Chicago Sun-Times* © 1996 and appear on pages 18, 20–21, 40–41, 51 (bottom). "Farewell to a Friend" by John H. White originally appeared in the November 17, 1996, edition of the *Chicago Sun-Times* and is used with permission.

Loyola Press
3441 North Ashland Avenue
Chicago, Illinois 60657

Printed in the United States of America

Library of Congress Cataloging-in-Publication Data
White, John H., 1945–
    The final journey : Joseph Cardinal Bernardin, 1928–1996 / photography of John H. White.
        p.   cm.
    ISBN 0-8294-0967-X (alk. paper)
    1. Bernardin, Joseph Louis, 1928–1996.   2. Cardinals–Illinois–Region–Biography.
    I. Title.
    BX4705.B   W   1997
    282' .092–dc21
    [B]   97-7387
                                          CIP

97 98 99 00 01 / 10 9 8 7 6 5 4 3 2 1

To the spirit of my dear friend Joseph Cardinal Bernardin.

Cardinal Bernardin's light, life, love, and spirit reflected the character of Jesus!
Let us follow his example!

—John H. White

1996
The Final Months

April 10	Reception of John Carroll Award from National Catholic Education Association, Philadelphia
April 26	Celebration of Cardinal's 30th Anniversary as a Bishop, 44th as a priest
June 1	Reception of Leon-Joseph Cardinal Suenens Award from John Carroll University, Cleveland
June 10	Reception of 1996 Humanitarian Award from the National Conference of Christians and Jews, Chicago Hilton and Towers
August 12	Press conference announcing Catholic Common Ground Project
August 30	Press conference announcing that his cancer has returned and is terminal
August 31	Anointing of the Sick, St. Barbara Church, Brookfield
September 9	Reception of Medal of Freedom at the White House followed by address at Georgetown University, Washington, D.C.
September 23–30	Rome: visit with Pope John Paul II
October 7	Prayer Service with Diocesan and Religious Priests, Holy Name Cathedral
October 24	Address on the Catholic Common Ground Project at the Sheraton Chicago
October 28	Pastoral visit to St. Queen of Angels Parish
October 29	Dedication of Cardinal Bernardin Cancer Center at Loyola Medical Center, Maywood
October 31	Entrusted day-to-day responsibilities of the Archdiocese to Vicar General, Bishop Raymond Goedert
November 1	Finished work on *The Gift of Peace*
November 14	Passed into eternal life

Contents

A Note to the Reader

We at Loyola Press have been deeply honored to work closely with Joseph Cardinal Bernardin and many of the talented men and women who knew him best.

In the summer of 1996 we released *This Man Bernardin,* by Pulitzer Prize-winning photojournalist John H. White and award-winning author Eugene Kennedy. The book, which stayed atop the Chicago bestseller list for many weeks and graces the personal libraries of thousands of people worldwide, documents Cardinal Bernardin's life and ministry from the time he was installed as Archbishop of Chicago in 1982 through 1995. The text and 180 duotone photographs, which include pictures from the Cardinal's family archives, reveal something of the essence of one of our nation's foremost religious leaders.

After working in close collaboration with the Cardinal himself during the final two months of his life, we had the distinct privilege of publishing Cardinal Bernardin's personal memoirs—*The Gift of Peace.* Since its release, *The Gift of Peace* has been a national bestseller and continues to provide spiritual guidance, insight, and comfort to hundreds of thousands of readers.

Now, Loyola Press proudly presents *The Final Journey.* This book is a tribute to the late Joseph Cardinal Bernardin that combines the photography and vision of John H. White with the words of some of those closest to the Cardinal—Bishop Raymond Goedert, Monsignor Kenneth Velo, Sister Mary Brian Costello, Sister Mary Lucia Skalka, Dr. Ellen Gaynor, and Mr. White.

While the photographs document the final year of the Cardinal's life, the written reflections help put these images into the broader context of a life dedicated to serving others as priest, bishop, archbishop, cardinal, friend, and brother.

The Final Journey marks the end of Cardinal Bernardin's earthly life and the beginning of his eternal life.

—*The Editors*

Farewell to a Friend
by John H. White

Sunday was the last time I saw him. I went to the residence about three o'clock in the afternoon. Monsignor Kenneth Velo took me upstairs to the Cardinal's library, where the Cardinal was resting on the couch. From time to time, his eyes would open briefly. While no words were spoken, I was keenly aware of a spiritual communication. We said what needed to be said. I saw a whole new meaning to the word *peace.* There comes a time when you just have to let go. There was no fear or holding back. He wasn't holding on here, and he wasn't rushing there.

It must have been a special parting because I'm not hurting now. It was comforting. When I walked out of there, I did not say goodbye, though I knew I would never see him again.

The greatest thing about him is this: He was a gift. He gave himself. When he first came to Chicago in 1982, he said, "For however many years I am given, I give myself to you. I offer you my service and leadership, my energies, my gifts, my mind, my heart, my strength, and, yes, my limitations. I offer you myself in faith, hope, and love." He was God's special gift to us. He fulfilled the promises he made on that August day when he embraced Chicago. He would come to define the word *shepherd.* His flock embraced him.

He was a teacher.

I was always struck by the importance of his hands and how he used them. He had a certain way of holding his hands in repose, and when he would give blessings. One of his trademarks was that when people would applaud, he would gesture with his hands for them to stop.

His eyes were truly windows to his soul. He hid no truth. His body changed with the wear of his illness, but the light of his eyes never changed. They mirrored his spirit and his peace. Many years ago, my brother, trying to explain life and death, gave me a passage of Scripture about understanding that we have two bodies: the physical body, which will break down and decay, and the spiritual body that is eternal, forever. That was another thing the Cardinal was trying to teach us. That there is religious hope. Death is not an end but a new existence. That's why he embraced it as his friend and tried to get us to understand the spirituality of new life.

He was completely credible. People would challenge him, "How can you tell someone about suffering?"

He'd say, "I have suffered."

They'd ask, "How can you tell someone about persecution?"

He'd say, "I have been persecuted."

How many times people would stop him on the street and tell him what they were going through. His eyes always communicated his concern and care. He did not always bless them or pray for them on the spot, but he would encourage them with a pat on the back or a handshake. Sometimes the most important thing he did was to listen.

Even people who perceived themselves as being totally outside his experience would soon find they had much in common. Every Christmas, he said Mass at Cook County Jail. Last year, he told the prisoners: "I am not here to judge you; neither is it within my power to set you free. But I can give you

Hands of Peace. They communicate so much about the
Cardinal. They were hands that greeted, hands that blessed,
and hands that bridged. These were hands that performed
the Holy Sacraments—and comforted condemned killers.
They spoke to us all.

another kind of freedom—the freedom that comes from being at peace with God, knowing that he loves us and will stand with us through life's trials.

"I know this inner peace from personal experience. Last June, when my doctors discovered that I had an aggressive cancer, the worst fears of my life suddenly became a reality. . . . Why do I share this with you this morning? Because I want you to know that from the very beginning of this illness I placed my life totally in God's hands, confident of his abiding love for me. And because of this I have experienced the deepest inner peace I have ever known.

"My dear brothers and sisters, I urge you this morning to place your lives in God's hands, confident that his love for you is abiding."

He always had a keen awareness of time, and of using his gift of time, prioritizing the priorities. And the last time I saw him, he still had a watch on. It was not a symbol that time was pressing him, or crushing him, but that time is a precious gift.

Some months ago, I stopped by his office and noticed his work, neatly organized, prioritized. One of the priorities was preparing his flock for his death. On August 30, he had told us that he had six months to a year. But in October, he learned that death would come sooner. He conserved his energy for a few projects: a major address at Georgetown University, finishing his book

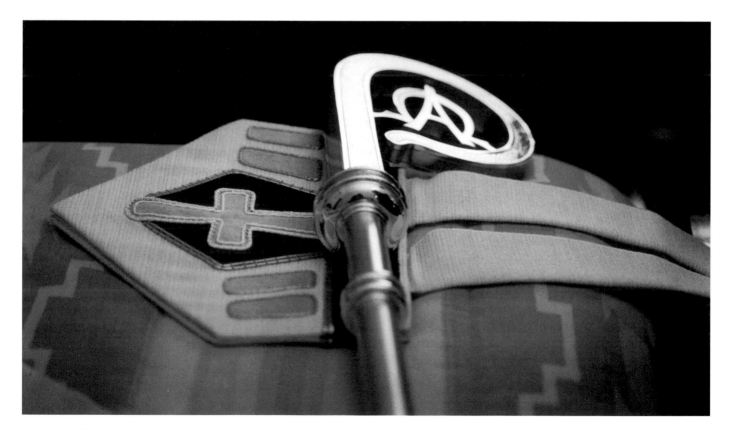

Symbols of a good shepherd. Cardinal Bernardin brought as much honor to the Archbishop's miter, crosier, and vestments as they brought to him.

about his last three years, and the dedication of the new Cardinal Bernardin Cancer Center at Loyola University Medical Center. As he finished his book, he wrote of fall changing to winter and winter to spring and new life. He was acknowledging that he wouldn't make it through the winter but that he was in transition to a new life.

I felt at the dedication of the cancer center that it would be his last public appearance because he did some things I'd never seen him do before. His hands, one folded over the other, were almost a trademark with him. That day, though, they spoke an emotion I had not seen before. They were not restless, but uncharacteristic. He held them in a different manner that I'd never seen him do before. After he blessed the crowd, the crowd blessed him in return. He bowed his head, and I felt a finality. Here was the person who had given and given and given, now ready to receive.

He gave me many gifts. The greatest was his friendship. He was a lamplighter. The lamp keeps burning, the light will always enlighten. It won't go out. His message has been the same all along. The soil it falls upon is different, more receptive. Now people will hear it.

His gifts to us continue and will multiply and magnify upon the lives and hearts of all he touched and who carry a touch, a memory, a ray of that light in our hearts. His gift of himself will fuel our journey with insight for the gift of life itself and a new relationship with this thing called death.

If there were something Cardinal Bernardin wanted to say to us now, I think it would be this passage from the apostle Paul:

"My dear friends, stand firm and don't be shaken. Always keep busy working for the Lord. For you know that everything you do for him is worthwhile."

I've watched the sun come up every morning for twenty years. My quiet time is alone in the morning at the lakefront. I listen and talk to God. I connect with the intrinsic spirit of life. The sky, the waves—nature speaks to me.

The sunrise Wednesday, as he lay dying, was quiet. It was not a big, fiery burst, but almost as if the sun said, "I'm not going to do that. I'm going to be quiet." There were ducks on the water, but they were moving quietly.

He died at 1:33 A.M. Thursday. Later that morning, I wanted to see how nature felt about the death of my friend. And there it spoke.

As long as I've been taking pictures of sunrises, I've never seen one more beautiful than Thursday's—a portrait of darkness and light represented pain and joy, a blend of changing, mostly vivid colors. But then through the thickness of the heavy clouds there appeared a ray of light—orange, red, its colors had no titles—for it was changing the darkness, not fighting its way into position, but rising into its natural place. Then, the beam suffused everything with its warmth, quiet, bright, luminous, and enlightening rays, and rose not just into the day but into the hearts of each of us. Thanks, I said. Thanks. It was like nature's billboard of peace and farewell. I felt the moment embracing the future with the special gift of peace.

John H. White

Laborer for the Lord
by Sr. Mary Brian Costello, R.S.M.

Sister Mary Brian Costello (pictured here with James J. O'Connor, Chairman and CEO Unicom Corporation) was the Cardinal's Chief of Staff. Her tireless devotion and energy paralleled the work of her boss.

From predawn on November 14, 1996, to dusk of November 20, a local Church and a whole metropolitan area struggled to find ways to absorb that most absolute of all human realities, the death of a beloved leader.

The headlines were there: "Chicago Mourns" and "Chicago Grieves a Man of Grace," but the experience of what the headlines meant would become a group effort over time. Thousands of caring persons searched for a personal way to say yes to this death, to "let go" and yet hold onto treasured memories.

Those days were filled with individual symbols of tribute—of remembering. Individuals gathered and became long lines of loving tribute and remembrance. It

seemed as if all of Chicagoland wanted to tell a personal experience of the Cardinal's influence, of that way he had of "belonging" to each one in a special way.

There was a kind of spontaneous "shrine" in front of the residence, the place that had been home to the Cardinal. Tokens of appreciation appeared: A child brought a flower; a woman set a lighted candle on the residence steps; someone slipped a poem that was a prayer onto the porch; others just knelt a moment in a kind of silent awe in the face of loss.

Day and night the lines formed around Holy Name Cathedral during the Cardinal's forty-two-hour wake. On Superior Street, on Wabash, down Chicago Avenue, across Rush, the lines became a remembering community, telling and retelling why they were there, keeping the life alive.

Remembering does that; it keeps the Cardinal present in the meaning his life has for us.

Joseph Cardinal Bernardin was such a presence that his absence could confound us, numb us. Remembering him keeps his spirit alive among us in a new relationship that expresses the unique meaning of his life.

It was my privilege to work with Cardinal Bernardin as Superintendent of Schools from 1984 until he appointed me to serve as his Chief of Staff in 1990. I learned so much and have so much to remember.

What will I remember?

I will remember the Cardinal as "Joseph the Worker."

Behind the public figure presiding at important events, behind the Prince of the Church, the Cardinal Archbishop, was Joseph the Worker.

Every day the Cardinal *worked.* He was self-disciplined in the extreme. His appointment calendar was exceedingly full, and he prepared carefully for his appointments and meetings. The appointments often required briefing time from staff and sometimes study or review the evening preceding the appointment.

Cardinal Bernardin maintained a voluminous correspondence. Hundreds of letters each week required his attention or response. He was most conscientious in this regard. Until the last week of his life, he struggled to find time to respond to requests for spiritual advice or assistance in some aspect of need. He worked to live his motto: "As Those Who Serve." How treasured now are his letters and signature!

Monsignor Kenneth Velo, in his funeral homily, asked, "Didn't he teach us?" One of the Cardinal's favorite teaching tools was the pastoral letter. He enjoyed the research, reading, and consultation that went into each pastoral. And he delighted in the drafting and redrafting of the document itself. The pursuit of each necessary comma, split infinitive, or dangling modifier was a personal enterprise for him. His pastoral letters carefully articulated his own perspectives and understandings of important Church teachings. His 1994 *Decisions* document gathered the input of more than eight thousand persons and led to his expression of how he intended to pursue the Church's mission in the years ahead. *Decisions* truly exemplified the way Cardinal Bernardin worked: listen, reflect, and pray, then teach.

The public saw the Cardinal at work in the many public appearances where his personal charisma drew hundreds to him. He loved to go to parishes and be with his people. He became the message he brought; he was the lesson he taught.

Often I have heard the Cardinal described as the Great Collaborator. I remember how costly it was for him to do all the work entailed to achieve that title: listening to diverse voices, weighing, and synthesizing, and then articulating in his artful manner a common ground. Joseph the worker.

Finally, I remember a very special Cardinal Bernardin. It is the memory of this unique leader in the Church who trusted women in significant leadership roles. I will always remember how he trusted me! How poignant I find it to remember that gentle voice say to me: "What should we do?" We! The memory of trust is a treasure. Instead of engaging in conflictual argumentation on women's rights, the Cardinal asked women to assume leadership roles in education, liturgy and divine worship, personnel management, and parish ministry. He trusted that in the final analysis, it was women and men serving collaboratively that would keep this church rooted in ground that was common—and holy.

Cardinal Bernardin has not "gone." He lives on in our memories of him, memorialized in the realization of his having left behind a local Church "more gentle, more loving, more compassionate."

A Person First, a Cardinal Second

by Sr. Mary Lucia Skalka, C.S.S.F.

The photo to the right and the now-famous photo of Cardinal Bernardin leaning on his crosier that graces the cover of this book are very special to me. Both photos were taken on May 25, 1996—my Jubilee celebrating fifty years since I entered the Felician order. The event was put on the Cardinal's calendar almost two years in advance to ensure that he would reserve that day to spend with me and the other Felician sisters. Yet, even with such careful preplanning, we still worried that the Cardinal would not be able to attend because of the trouble he was having with his back and all that he had gone through with his cancer treatment. We prayed that God would give him the strength to be with us on that day.

Cardinal Bernardin greatly honored me by being part of my Jubilee; it was his way of showing appreciation for our friendship and the fourteen years I served as his cook at the residence. In his homily at Mass that day he told us he felt a part of our group and shared in my celebration by pointing out that he entered the priesthood at the same time I entered the Felician order.

When I think of Cardinal Bernardin, I think of someone who was very approachable, warm, understanding, and loving. I think of a sincere, genuine human being.

He was "just" an Archbishop when I first met him—newly appointed to head the Archdiocese of Chicago after serving as Archbishop of Cincinnati for the previous ten years. In his first week in Chicago he asked his friend, Father Alvin Zugelter, who had moved with him from Cincinnati, to maintain the residence and handle assembling a full-time staff. Father Zugelter, upon learning that some of the sisters from my order had helped Cardinal Cody when he hosted the Holy Father during his visit to the United States in 1979, contacted our provincial, Sister Mary Laudiose Karbal, and asked her to select three sisters to help the new Archbishop. I was chosen to prepare the meals and help around the house.

When I first arrived at the residence I told Archbishop Bernardin, "Don't expect much from me, I'm just plain simple Lucia." Afterward he came into the kitchen, sat down, and said, "I suppose you are wondering what my likes and dislikes are." I said, "yes." He smiled and said, "I eat everything," then he told me there were only a few foods he could not tolerate. He was very disciplined in all aspects of his life. When it came to food, he maintained a consistent and balanced diet.

One of Archbishop Bernardin's first priorities was to turn his house into a home. He tore down the fence that had surrounded the residence and created a friendly relationship with his neighbors. He asked that there be flowers and a garden in the yard. He also made all who lived and worked in the house feel like part of a family. My kitchen always contributed to the family atmosphere; for example, Cardinal Bernardin would stop in after work to see what I was cooking and taste various dishes that were being prepared. He would also suggest recipes, especially for Italian meals, for me to try. If he liked any particular recipe he would say, "Don't put that one too far away."

The day of the Jubilee: Sister Mary Lucia Skalka with her special guest. Cardinal Bernardin honored Sister Lucia by attending her fifty-year anniversary since entering the Felician order. Sister Lucia cooked for Cardinal Bernardin after he arrived in Chicago as "just" an archbishop in 1982.

I also loved storing leftovers in the refrigerator for priests and guests who liked late-night snacks. People were free to come and go as they wished.

Soon after coming to Chicago, Archbishop Bernardin was made a Cardinal. But titles never affected him; he was always a human being first. He was very appreciative of the things people did for him, especially during the last three years of his life. I will always cherish the special friendship I shared with the Cardinal. He was a prayerful man who served others until the end of his life. And his life and ministry will continue to nourish the lives of people everywhere.

Prescription for Life
by Dr. Ellen Gaynor, O.P., M.D.

Dr. Ellen Gaynor with her patient at the October 29, 1996, naming of the Cardinal Bernardin Cancer Center at Loyola University Medical Center in Maywood, Illinois.

I had the great privilege this past year of being Cardinal Joseph Bernardin's oncologist. I found early on that I was strongly drawn to him. Why? Perhaps it was his kindness, his gentleness. On each of his visits to the Loyola Cancer Center, I would meet him at the door, and frequently thought, "I know exactly how the disciples of Jesus must have felt as they tried to control the crowds." The patients at the center flocked to the Cardinal, and to each he would say, "It's so good to see you. I will pray for you." I recall one occasion when he came because the pain in his back had become excruciating. My only thought was to move him as quickly as possible into an examining room. His only thought seemed to be to greet the many people who stopped him as we walked down the corridor.

Cardinal Bernardin had a special ministry to the sick during the last year of his life. I cannot tell you how often a patient would say to me, "Dr. Gaynor, guess who wrote to me?" as he or she gave me an envelope whose letterhead had become very familiar, the Office of the Archbishop of Chicago. But this was more than just a letter from the Cardinal; this was a letter from a soulmate, a friend who understood what the patient was going through.

Yes, I was drawn to the man because of his kindness and gentleness, but there was something more, his sharp mind, his subtle humor. Many times I would find myself engaged in a detailed conversation about such topics as osteoporosis or spinal stenosis, and I would say to myself, "Why am I telling him all this?" Because not only did he want to know, but he immediately comprehended what I was talking about. And I learned early on that I could get away with nothing—his questions struck like arrows at the heart of whatever issue was on the table.

Like many patients, he did not like taking medicine. He would delight in calling me before a trip to tell me he had packed all of his pills into just *one* extra suitcase. As a physician, it annoys me when patients refer to medications not by name, but by size, shape, or color. Cardinal Bernardin knew as well as I knew the name and dosage of every drug he ever took, yet he frequently referred to them by their size or color. In the several weeks before his death, he took Benadryl. Before he started using it, I didn't realize it was a "red pill." But he informed me, and in all subsequent conversations we referred to it as the "red pill." One night, shortly before he died, I asked him to take two of the red pills at bedtime. He said to me, "Ellen, may I share something with you? Benadryl also comes as a blue pill, and my new supply is blue." On more than one subsequent occasion, I was gently—so very gently—corrected when I said, "take two of the red pills" and he replied, "you mean blue pills."

Yes, I was drawn to this man because of his sharp mind and his quick wit. But there was something more, his honesty, his courage, his great faith. The only thing he asked of me was that I be honest with him. There were many times when it was so hard to honor his request. On August 28, he had what we thought would be a routine MRI to document that his cancer was in remission. When I told him his cancer had recurred, his first statement was, "This changes everything." His second was, "Now I will have the chance to put into practice what I have been telling patients all year—death is my friend." When he asked how long he had to live, I told him a year or less.

In early October, he had another MRI that showed disease progression, and I told him his life expectancy was considerably less. He called me that evening and said, "This has been a hard day. I am processing what you have told me. But I want you to know that I am all right." He assumed that he would be able to work through December. As we moved through October, it became clear that his strength was deteriorating rapidly, and on the day he announced he was turning over the responsibilities of running the Archdiocese, I said to him, "You are on November 1 where you thought you would be on January 1." He replied simply that he knew.

When I saw Cardinal Bernardin on the Friday before his death, he asked me if he would live until Christmas. I told him that I was certain he would die before Christmas. He said simply, "I am ready." I promised I would tell him when he was very close to death—I thought he would live to see Thanksgiving. When I saw him three days later, there had been a very rapid deterioration that I had not expected. I said to him, "Cardinal Bernardin, you are very close— you will die this week." I asked him, "Are you okay with this?" to which he replied, "If it must be . . . I am ready."

I stand in awe of this man. Inner peace such as Cardinal Bernardin displayed does not just happen, it has to be nurtured over a lifetime. But there was something more. In speaking to the priests of the Archdiocese last year, the Cardinal had said, "Men and women everywhere have a deep desire to come in contact with the transcendent. That's what ordinary people want. I believe that with all my heart."

I have been on a very difficult journey— for the seventeen months I was the Cardinal's doctor and following his death—but now I understand who this man Bernardin was and why I was so drawn to him. This was a man who actually put on Christ in his own life. In this man, Bernardin, we experienced the transcendent—we experienced our God.

Lasting Images

The seat of the Archbishop. The Cardinal always considered
himself an ordinary man in an extraordinary position.

As a leader, the Cardinal stood out.
As a priest, he blended with the crowd.

In the time before he discovered his cancer had returned after being in remission for fifteen months, the Cardinal tirelessly celebrated Masses throughout the Archdiocese.

"The Cancer Has Returned"

AUGUST 30, 1996, PRESS CONFERENCE

by Joseph Cardinal Bernardin

Since I was diagnosed as having pancreatic cancer last June and, later, various spinal difficulties, I have kept everyone fully apprised of my health. In keeping with that policy I come to you again today to give you an update.

On Wednesday of this week, examinations conducted at Loyola Medical Center indicated that the cancer has returned, this time in the liver. I have been told that it is terminal and my life expectancy is one year or less. I will indeed begin a different form of chemotherapy entitled Gemzar (gemcitabine). If successful, this therapy may increase my time somewhat but it will not effect a cure.

In light of this latest diagnosis, the back surgery for the spinal stenosis has been cancelled. Such surgery is usually done only when the prospects for life are more promising. Moreover, were the surgery to take place, it would delay the chemotherapy.

I have been assured that I still have some quality time left. My prayer is that I will use whatever time is left in a positive way, that is, in a way that will be of benefit to the priests and people I have been called to serve, as well as to my own spiritual well-being.

Over the past year, I have counseled the cancer patients with whom I have been in touch (the prayer list now numbers over 600) to place themselves entirely in the hands of the Lord. I have personally always tried to do that; now I have done so with greater conviction and trust than ever before. While I know that, humanly speaking, I will have to deal with difficult moments, I can say in all sincerity that I am at peace. I consider this as God's special gift to me at this moment in my life.

There is another thought I have shared with my friends who have cancer and I would like to share with you; indeed it follows from what I have just said. We can look at death as an enemy or a friend. If we see it as an enemy, death causes anxiety and fear. We tend to go into a state of denial. But if we see it as a friend, our attitude is truly different. As a person of faith, I see death as a friend, as the transition from earthly life to life eternal.

In the coming months I will continue to serve the Archdiocese in the way I have in the past. I will keep a full schedule for as long as I can. Moreover, as appropriate, I will keep everyone informed of my health.

In conclusion, I wish to speak two brief words. First, to my priests and people whom I love so much. Pray that I may continue to serve you and the broader Church with understanding, compassion, and fidelity. Through our solidarity and mutual support and trust, may we give a credible witness to God's love for all of us.

My second word is to you, the members of the media. We have enjoyed a good professional relationship in the years I have been Archbishop of Chicago—and this will continue. Now I ask that you stand with me personally. Whatever your religious affiliation may be, I ask that you say a prayer for me. And, in return, I will pray for you and your loved ones.

The Cardinal tells a room packed with photographers and reporters, "You are my family." He wanted the news media to help him teach his lessons on dying. "Now I ask that you stand with me personally. Whatever your religious affiliation may be, I ask that you say a prayer for me. And, in return, I will pray for you and your loved ones."

One day after the announcement, the Cardinal attends a ceremony for the anointing of the sick at Saint Barbara's Church in Brookfield, Illinois.

Cardinal Bernardin was anointed
first by Bishop Raymond Goedert.
Then he joined Goedert
and other priests in blessing
hundreds of people

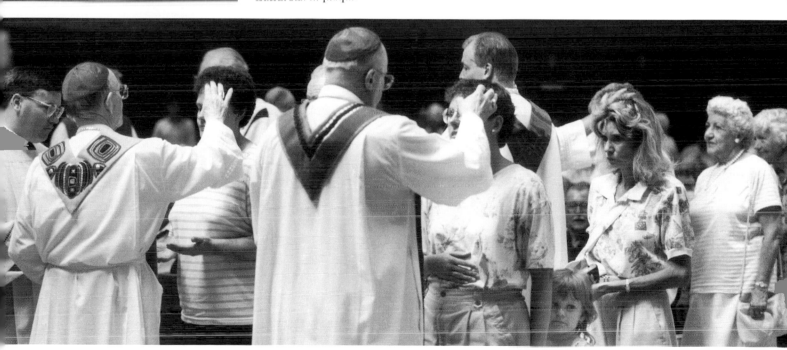

On September 9, Cardinal Bernardin receives the Presidential Medal of Freedom at a White House ceremony. "As the Archbishop of Chicago, Joseph Cardinal Bernardin is one of our nation's most beloved men and one of Catholicism's great leaders," said President Clinton. "When others have pulled people apart, Cardinal Bernardin has sought common ground." As the president embraced the Cardinal, Clinton wiped away a tear.

Later in the day, the Cardinal and his proud sister, Elaine Addison, visit an old friend, Georgetown University President Leo O'Donovan. Back pain failed to slow the Cardinal. This was the only moment of leisure for Bernardin in a day that included several interviews and a major address at the university. "It was a very full, exhausting day—but one of the most memorable in my life," he later wrote in his memoirs.

September 12: Three days later, as his grueling Washington trip drew to a close, one could see physical changes taking place. The Cardinal, pictured above with Anthony Cardinal Bevilacqua and Bernard Cardinal Law, later wrote, "I was glad I brought my cane with me." The cardinals placed themselves in front of the Capitol and took issue with President Clinton's policy on abortion.

Before returning to Chicago, Bernardin helped celebrate a Mass marking the fiftieth anniversary of James Cardinal Hickey's entrance into the priesthood. As the ceremony was about to begin, Bernardin and his fellow U.S. cardinals posed for a photo *(top right)*—their last one together. They are (from left): The Most Reverend Agostino Cacciavillan; Cardinals William Keeler, Anthony Bevilacqua, Edmund Szoka, Joseph Bernardin, James Hickey, William Baum, Bernard Law, Roger Mahony, and Adam Maida; and Bishop Anthony M. Pilla.

The newly named Cardinal Bernardin Cancer Center is dedicated October 29 at Loyola University Medical Center in Maywood, just west of Chicago. The Center was where Bernardin had previously been treated for pancreatic cancer. From the balcony of the atrium, Cardinal Bernardin blessed the audience—and they returned the blessing. Those with the Cardinal are (from left to right) Frank Considine, Chairman of the Board of Directors for Loyola University Health System; Dr. Richard J. Fisher, Director of the Center; Father John J. Piderit, S.J., President of Loyola University; Dr. Ellen Gaynor, O.P., the Cardinal's oncologist; and Anne R. McCall, his radiologist.

The Loyola dedication is the Cardinal's final public appearance.
Reporters told him that he looked good, but Bernardin warned that
appearances can be misleading. The Cardinal seemed to be holding
his emotions inside, but his hands told the story.

"Our brother Joseph is at peace. His life on earth has ended. Cardinal Bernardin passed away this morning at 1:33 A.M. As Christians, we believe that Cardinal Bernardin at long last begins a new life, an everlasting life, with our Lord Jesus. We believe that today he will meet his Redeemer face to face."

—*Statement of Bishop Raymond Goedert, Nov. 14, 1996.*

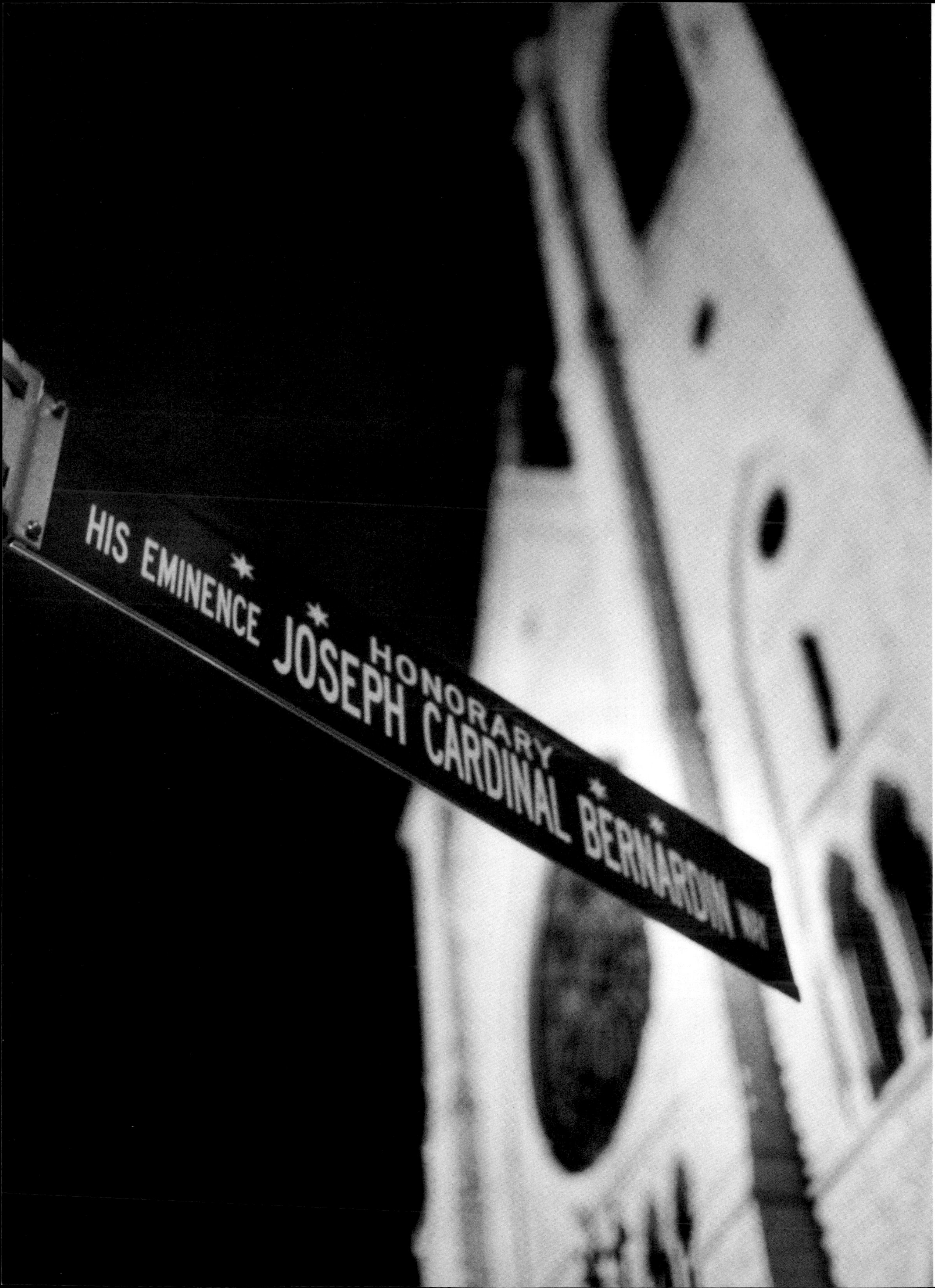
HONORARY
HIS EMINENCE JOSEPH CARDINAL BERNARDIN WAY

One final gift. The Cardinal planned his own farewell, allowing time for all of Chicago to pay its last respects at Holy Name Cathedral on Chicago's Near North Side.

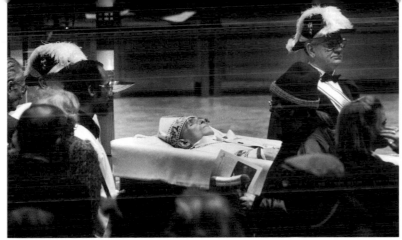

Thousands of people file into the Cathedral to visit the casket of Cardinal Bernardin during the forty-two-hour wake. They came at all hours of the day and night.

On November 19, one day before the funeral, a special service was offered for the priests of the Archdiocese. In his fourteen years as Archbishop, Bernardin formed a special bond with his priests. He once said, "The first prayer I say each day is for the priests." Father Scott Donahue *(left, seated)* was chosen by the Cardinal to give the homily at the service. Hundreds of priests and seminarians filled Holy Name Cathedral.

Jesus Christ is the light of the world,
The light no darkness can overcome.
Stay with us, Lord, for it is evening.
And the day is almost over.
Let your light scatter the darkness.
And illumine your church.

Cardinal Bernardin reached out to all faiths—
and all faiths reached out to him. Religious lead-
ers from all over the city were invited to the
Cathedral to mourn for their brother. Rabbi
Herman Schaalman *(below)* led a Jewish memo-
rial. Greek Orthodox Bishop Iakavos, Auxiliary
Bishop Timothy Lyne, retired Episcopal Bishop
James Montgomery, and Evangelical Lutheran
Bishop Kenneth Olsen gathered for an ecumeni-
cal prayer service.

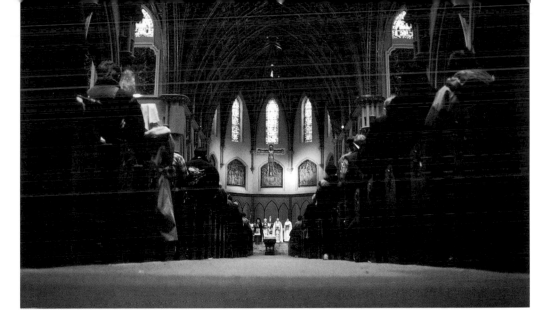

Moments before the Mass of
Christian Burial, the casket is
closed and covered. Holy Name
Cathedral was never more
quiet.

"Cardinal. Eminence. You're Home. You're Home."

NOVEMBER 20, 1996, FUNERAL MASS HOMILY

by Rev. Msgr. Kenneth Velo

Whether you are in the first pew or the thirtieth pew of this great cathedral; whether you are participating through the public-address system or seated in the auditorium; whether you are listening on the radio as you travel the Dan Ryan Expressway or sitting in a kitchen in Rogers Park; whether you are watching television coverage of this funeral service in a nursing home in Waukegan, a living room in Calumet City, or a classroom on Chicago's West Side; today, this day, you are all dignitaries, for God has touched you through the life of Cardinal Bernardin; and I greet you as family and friends.

Perhaps you are wondering who I am. Let me introduce myself in the way that Mrs. Bernardin, the Cardinal's 92-year-old mother, knows me. I am Father Velo, the "regular driver."

And one of the greatest compliments His Eminence paid me through the years was just to fall asleep in the car. We would travel the city's streets and sometimes make phone calls, but he would usually fall asleep towards the end of our journey. I would say, "Cardinal, we're here. We've arrived." The comb would come out of his pocket, and the event, the ceremony, the dinner—whatever—would begin, but not before he said to me, "Our objective is to get out of here as quickly as possible."

Somewhere over Greenland in mid September, His Eminence showed me his funeral plans. I began to cry. I saw the things that he had listed. I saw my name. I saw the name of Cardinal Mahony, whom he asked to celebrate this Mass of Christian Burial. I saw the name of another close good friend, Father Donahue, whom he asked to deliver the homily at the prayer service for priests. As I cried, he said, "Don't worry. I have cried, too."

I was somewhat fearful, but I think the homily of this Mass has been given over these past months of illness, through the forgiveness he gave to all sorts of people and through his life of service and ministry. That being said, let us begin.

It was here in this pulpit on October 7 that the Cardinal addressed his priests. He talked about Jesus. He told us that Jesus was a person of integrity, one who was loved and loving, that Jesus was patient, that Jesus was a teacher. His friends saw him experience an excruciating death, and they were locked in the Upper Room for fear. They, perhaps, were fearful of the limitations they had—what would happen to them?

They were fearful because they just did not understand everything he had to say. Then Jesus came. He showed them his hands and his side. He stood in their midst and said, "Peace be with you, my peace I give to you." And these missionaries were sent forth to proclaim the gospel, and they did. So much so, that we have heard the gospel message of the Lord Jesus and gather this day. You can imagine what it was like for them. They must have been nudging themselves, saying, "Didn't he teach us? Didn't he show us the way?"

At one of Cardinal Bernardin's final Masses, Monsignor Velo helps his dear friend put on his vestments.

Cardinal Bernardin was many things to people, but, most of all, he was a teacher. He taught lessons of life, and I would like to talk about Cardinal Bernardin in the context of one of his favorite prayers, a prayer he kept in the pocket of his suit and used at all sorts of different times. It is the Prayer of St. Francis of Assisi.

April 2, 1928: *Lord, make me an instrument of your peace.* Joseph Bernardin was born in South Carolina, the oldest of two children, to Joseph and Maria Simion Bernardin. His father died when Joseph was six. Thus, he found, even at that early age, that he had to deal with responsibility. He wore the trousers of the family, even though they were short pants.

In South Carolina at that time, there were few Italians and very few Catholics. He bridged the gap. He united himself with family and friends. There was no difference. He was a loyal son, and that loyalty continued, so much so, that he would visit his mother each and every day that he was able.

He united the bonds of his family between those who were in this country and those who were in Italy. And so we say, Mrs. Bernardin (joined with us in spirit in the care of the Little Sisters of the Poor) Elaine, Jim, Anna Marie, Jimmy, Joseph, Angela, cousins from Columbia and Philadelphia, *cugini d'Italia, di Primiero vicino le montagne Dolemiti:* Didn't he teach us? Didn't he show us the way?

April 26, 1952: *Lord, make me an instrument of your peace.* Joseph Bernardin was ordained for the Church of Charleston. He

was a high school teacher, a chaplain. He held all sorts of diocesan offices. He knew what small rural missions were like. And his best days were doing the pastoral work with the responsibility he held. In eight years he had four bishops. He said he would uphold the apostolic succession. He was a man of faith and fidelity. People of God in Charleston: Didn't he teach us? Didn't he show us the way?

April 26, 1966: *Lord, make me an instrument of your peace.* He was consecrated a bishop, the youngest in the country. His friends said he was a "boy bishop." And he would serve the Church of Atlanta as Vicar General and pastor of Christ the King Cathedral. But most of all, he assisted Archbishop Hallinan and learned from him. Those years were filled with all sorts of meetings about race relations, and he became a leader of ecumenism. People of Atlanta: Didn't he teach us? Didn't he show us the way?

April 10, 1968: *Lord, make me an instrument of your peace.* Bishop Bernardin became General Secretary of the National Conference of Catholic Bishops. He was to organize the new Conference. He was a leader *par excellence.* Elected to many positions, he represented the bishops of this country at every Synod of Bishops since then. He brought people together. He worked hard at doing that. He had the gift of resilience. While on a trip with some of his bishop friends, he took a moped and went out. There was an accident. They found him in brambles and thorns, with the wheels turning up and around, and he said, "I finally got the knack of it!"

He was a unifier. Bishops and staff of the National Conference of Catholic Bishops: Didn't he teach us? Didn't he show us the way?

November 21, 1972: *Lord, make me an instrument of your peace.* He was called to serve the Church of Cincinnati. Once more,

he basked in the pastoral realm; there he was able to implement those wonderful documents of Vatican II. He was a pastor with his priests and people. He visited the jail and set up times to do that. He followed new developments in ministry. He reorganized the Archdiocese. It was during those years that he deepened his spiritual life in the Lord Jesus. People of Cincinnati: Didn't he teach us? Didn't he show us the way?

It was on August 25, 1982, the prayer again: *Lord, make me an instrument of your peace.* In this darkened cathedral and darkened Archdiocese, he brought the light of Christ. As Father Donahue spoke so eloquently last night, he brought light and life that continue this day. Yes, it was joy and pardon, faith and hope, and much more light that he brought to us. If you do not think so, read our papers, watch our television news. See the faces of the people standing in line this past week to make a final visitation to their Archbishop.

He taught us to respect others. He made us proud of being priests while recognizing and affirming emerging ministries in the Church.

He was a man of humility. He told of being on vacation. He was far away from Chicago, dressed in casual clothes, walking the aisles of a grocery store to prepare for the evening meal. A man saw him. "Oh, I can't believe you're here. Do you have one minute? Do you have one minute to see my wife? She's out in the parking lot. Do you have one minute?"

The Cardinal—saying to himself, "He recognized me"—walked down the aisle, through the grocery store turnstile, and into the parking lot. The man said, "My car is over there. There's my wife." The Cardinal walked up to the car. The man said, "Helen, look who's here! Dr. Kresnick!"

People know him now! They know him, and they love him. What a presence he had in this Church of Chicago! To the people

The priests of the Archdiocese bless their brother Joseph during the funeral Mass.

of Lake and Cook Counties; to you, my brothers and sisters who are part of this great Archdiocese: Didn't he teach us? Didn't he show us the way?

He took hard stands: the consistent ethic of life, nuclear disarmament, health care for the poor, racial injustice. He stood on the U.S. Capitol steps against partial-birth abortions. And in his last days, during his own suffering, he spoke out loudly and clearly to the U.S. Supreme Court about assisted suicide. Leaders of government, people of good will everywhere: Didn't he teach us? Didn't he show us the way?

In the Church and among leaders of other religions, he took initiatives. He had a difficult time with people who directed lives by using rearview mirrors. He wanted people to come around the table and to see, not what divides us, but what brings us together. He wanted to make common ground, holy ground. Leaders of the Church, pick up the torch of Jesus, of John XXIII, of Joseph Bernardin, that all may be one. Didn't he teach us? Didn't he show us the way?

Every day, in the quiet of his chapel when we were privileged to celebrate the Eucharist, there was always one prayer at the conclusion of his Prayer of the Faithful, and, I am sure, throughout his first hour of prayer in his study. He prayed for an increase of vocations to the priesthood and the religious life. There are many boys and girls, young men and women, who are listening as we speak this very moment. You see how fulfilling and satisfying his life was, and how yours could be. As you walk through your life in service to others, think about that in response to his prayer of service to the Church, and you will not regret it. Young men and women, through his life: Didn't he teach us? Didn't he show us the way?

He put himself into everything. He would awaken very early in the morning and spend his first hour in prayer. He seldom said no. He would write thank-you letters for thank-you letters! He would give himself

to priests and people. Those who worked on the fourth floor of the Pastoral Center saw the care in which he greeted visitors. Troubled people felt so proud when they walked out of his office. And even when most people would have gone on disability after the news of cancer, our friend started a new ministry and reached out to cancer patients with notes and phone calls and visits and prayer. Priest once more, he knew it is in giving that we receive.

Oh, there were many trials in life. There were protesters around the cathedral so often. Fortunately, he was able to see those same protesters come down about a mile to his residence for prayer vigils during these last few months.

He made difficult decisions. Yes, I was with him when he was snubbed by some. He made a visit to Stateville, which many of us will never forget, to an inmate near his hour of death. But at the same time he wrote to victims, showing sensitivity and care. And who will ever be able to forget that false accusation? But, hopefully, let us never forget his forgiveness, the Cardinal's forgiveness, from the very first moment, and that wonderful reconciliation of which he spoke time and time again. For, he knew that it is in pardoning that we are pardoned.

I was with him in the examining room when he was told by Dr. Furey that he had an aggressive form of cancer. The doctor said it would most likely be his life-ending event. I was there, too, when his oncologist, Dr. Gaynor, told him that the cancer was back after fourteen months of remission. In those situations, he calmly dealt with this, for he was embracing a friend. Yes, he was embracing death as a friend. For, he knew that it is in dying that we are born to eternal life.

Yes, the Cardinal was very, very special. Even to say he was a great man, a great priest, or a great bishop does not adequately say who he has been for us. The words of description are insufficient. All we can do is gather around God's altar to give thanks for his life

Moments after Monsignor Velo's homily, the congregation kneels as cardinals and bishops consecrate the Eucharist.

and ministry, thanks for what he meant to each and every one of us, thanks for what he was to countless people in this area, and what he was to people across this beautiful land and, yes, around the world.

It was in 1982 that we gathered here, the priests of this Archdiocese, the lay ministers and people of this Church. Our hearts were locked out of fear of the unknown. What would this new shepherd be like? He came and stood in our midst as one who served and said, "Peace be with you. Christ's peace I leave with you."

These past three years, we have gathered around television sets and radios, water coolers and family tables. Our hearts were locked out of fear. We heard about accusations. We heard about his cancer. We heard about how he was going to die. But through press conferences—many of them—through prayer services, through events, ceremonies,

and gatherings, he came among us as one who served and said, "Peace be with you. Christ's peace I leave with you."

And in the early hours of Thursday morning, November 14, shortly after friends gathered around his deathbed as Cardinal Mahony ministered to us, we viewed his casket being carried from his residence on North State Parkway—our hearts locked in pain. But as we gather this day, he comes to us as God's instrument to say, "Peace be with you. Christ's peace I leave with you."

I know there are many people watching, listening, standing with us at this hour. But I ask you to allow me just a few words with the Cardinal. You see, it has been a long, long and beautiful ride.

Cardinal. Eminence. You're home. You're home.

November 20: As the Cardinal's funeral procession passed through the streets of Chicago, people's love and admiration were expressed in many ways. The sign of the cross moved through the crowd person to person—keeping pace with the hearse. From the Gold Coast to the West Side and the suburbs, people rang bells, prayed silently, or simply watched. It was as if they were all part of the same orchestra. Even in death, the Cardinal brought people together.

The public event becomes a private moment. After days of ceremony, the Cardinal is laid to rest inside the Bishops' Mausoleum at Mount Carmel Cemetery in Hillside. The Cardinal's sister, Elaine Addison, is held by her husband, James, as other members of Bernardin's extended "family" look on.

"A Badge of Honor"

December 14, 1996,
Month's Mind Mass Homily
by Most Rev. Raymond E. Goedert, D.D.

Bishop Raymond Goedert took the helm of the Archdiocese of Chicago from October 31 until the appointment of the new Archbishop.

It's hard to believe that a month has passed by already since the death of our brother Joseph. The memory of all events surrounding his final weeks, his death, his funeral, are still so fresh in our minds.

Over these past four weeks we have found ourselves weeping and worrying, reminiscing and offering thanks—our emotions have truly run the full gamut. But now, in a sense, the intensity of the storm has subsided. Everything is growing calmer. Like the disciples in today's gospel, we see that the boat is still afloat. We have not drowned in our grief. The Lord has not abandoned us; on the contrary, he has walked with us every inch of the way as we accompanied Joseph to the gate. And

today, with "hope that draws its life from the resurrection of Jesus Christ," we stand in awe with our memories of the life and the death of Joseph Cardinal Bernardin.

If I were to identify the emotion that stands out for me above all the others as a result of the journey Joseph and we have just completed, I believe I can sum it up in just one word—*pride!*

Pride, first of all, in Joseph. What a man! What a priest! What a bishop! When Father Jerry Boland summed it up on the eve of the funeral, how right he was when he said: "Joseph, you were the best!" And who will ever forget the standing ovation that the priests gave Joseph that night? It will continue to resound within our hearts for as long as we live. It was our way of saying: "Joseph, we love you. You have truly been our brother. You have taught us so much. We are so very proud of you!"

And we thank Joseph, too, for having restored pride in our priesthood, pride in our Catholic faith. Both have taken a beating in recent years, but over and over again in these last few months of Joseph's life, have you not heard priests say that they have never felt so good about their priesthood? The Roman collar has become once again a badge of honor! And haven't you heard your friends say how proud they were to be Catholics as they watched the ceremonies of the funeral liturgies unfold on their television screens? Haven't you said it yourself? Haven't you experienced tears of joy and gratitude for your faith, as you witnessed the cortege winding its way through the streets of Chicago? Wasn't your heart thrilled as you saw silent mourners standing as a guard of honor along Michigan Avenue—ordinary people waving and kneeling as Joseph's body moved down the boulevard—firemen standing at attention alongside their engines as the procession passed them by? Yes, Joseph, you restored to us a pride that has eluded us for a long, long time.

And now, in a little while we will be elevating his *galero*—his red hat—to the ceiling of this Cathedral. It will hang in honor alongside those of Mundelein, Stritch, Meyer, and Cody. In a way, the scene will be somewhat reminiscent of those final moments of Christ's life on earth. As he ascended into the heavens, his disciples who were mesmerized by his departure were gently chided by the angels for standing around in awe, not knowing just what they were supposed to do. Christ's death and resurrection calls us to action. And so does that of our brother, Joseph.

Joseph Bernardin, as you well know, was not one to stand around idle. He was a prodigious worker, skilled administrator, excellent mediator, priest, and bishop *par excellence*. And this is the message that I take from the liturgy today. This is truly a *celebration*. As we heard from Peter in the first reading: "There is cause for rejoicing here." The time for grieving has officially ended, but hopefully the impact of Joseph's life will continue to be felt in the ministry of each one of us who have found new energy in the example he has given us. His faith, which he upheld to the very last breath of his life, must continue to inspire us to live out our own faith with renewed enthusiasm. It is now our turn to pick up where he left off—to love Our Lord and our people with all our hearts, with all our minds, with all our strength.

Joseph Bernardin was your brother and mine. He believed with all his heart that we are all brothers and sisters in Jesus Christ. What a legacy he has left us! May we embrace it, and may we live it to the fullest!

December 14: One month after the Cardinal's death, his ceremonial, red hat—or *galero*—is raised on ropes to the ceiling at Holy Name Cathedral. In the front row were (from left) Dr. Ellen Gaynor; Sister Mary Lucia Skalka; Father Scott Donahue; F. Octavie Mosimann, the Cardinal's secretary; and Monsignor Kenneth Velo. The Cardinal's journey to heaven is complete, but his *galero* remains bound to earth as a physical reminder of one of Chicago's most beloved leaders.

Prayer of Saint Francis

Lord, make me an instrument of your peace.
Where there is hatred . . . let me sow **love.**
Where there is injury . . . **pardon.**
Where there is discord. . . **unity.**
Where there is doubt . . . **faith.**
Where there is error. . . **truth.**
Where there is despair . . . **hope.**
Where there is sadness . . . **joy.**
Where there is darkness . . . **light.**
O Divine Master, grant that I may not so much seek.
To be consoled . . . as to **console.**
To be understood . . . as to **understand.**
To be loved . . . as to **love.**
                          for
It is in giving . . . that we **receive.**
It is in pardoning . . . that we are **pardoned.**
It is in dying . . . that we are born to **eternal life.**

—**Saint Francis of Assisi**